# Microsoft Visio 2013

# Basics

### Tutorial Books

# Contents

# Introduction

Welcome to the *Visio 2013 Basics* book. This book is written to assist students, planners, and IT professionals in create diagram, chart, and plans. It covers the important features and functionalities of Visio 2013 using relevant examples and exercises.

This book is written for new users, who can use it as a self-study resource to learn Visio 2013. In addition, it can also be used as a reference for experienced users. This book is focused on creating basic flowcharts, brainstorming diagrams, organization charts, pivot diagram, timelines, calendars, and detailed network diagrams.

## Topics covered in this Book

"Getting Started with Visio 2013", introduces Microsoft Visio 2013. The user interface and terminology are discussed in this section.

Tutorial 1, "Creating Basic Flow Charts", teaches you to create basic diagrams using Visio stencils.

Tutorial 2, "Validating Diagrams", teaches you to check the diagrams for any errors.

Tutorial 3, "Applying Themes to Diagrams", shows you change the appearance of the diagram by applying various themes, colors, and background.

Tutorial 4, "Publishing your Diagrams", teaches you to print diagrams.

Tutorial 5, "Creating Brainstorming Diagram", teaches you to create brainstorming diagrams.

Tutorial 6, "Creating Organizational Charts", teaches you to create organizational charts.

Tutorial 7, "Creating Organizational Charts using Wizard", teaches you to create an organizational chart by entering data in an excel sheet.

Tutorial 8, "Creating Organizational Charts using External Data", teaches you to create an organizational chart using an existing data. It also shows you to link data to shapes.

Tutorial 9, "Creating Pivot Diagrams", covers how to create Pivot diagrams using an existing data.

Tutorial 10, "Creating Calendars", covers how to create calendars and add events.

Tutorial 11, "Creating Timelines", covers how to create project timelines.

Tutorial 12, "Creating Detailed Network Diagrams", covers how to create network diagrams.

# Getting Started with Visio 2013

## Introduction to Visio 2013

Visio 2013 is a software programme for presenting the information in a graphical manner. You can create professional diagrams, drawings and other graphical data related to engineering, business, networking, software, and other fields. Visio 2013 makes it easy to capture your ideas graphically, and then modify them frequently. In addition to that, you can create drawings with great accuracy.

## Templates available in Visio 2013

Visio 2013 offers many templates to carry out different types of diagrams. For example, Visio 2013 provides you with the **Organization Chart** template to create good-looking organizational diagrams. Likewise, there are many templates to create diagrams such as architectural plans, flow charts, calendars, network diagrams, electrical diagrams, brainstorming diagrams and so on.

## Starting Visio 2013

To start Visio 2013, click the **Visio 2013** icon on the windows grid.   The Backstage appears as shown. You can select different types of templates from the Backstage to start new drawing.

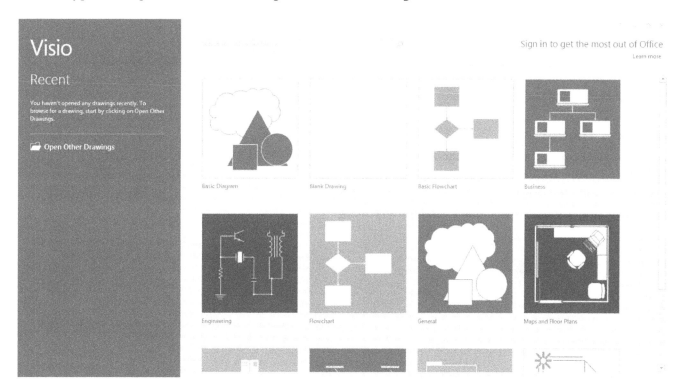

## Starting a New Blank Drawing

Click the **Blank Drawing** template on the initial screen, and then select the units of measurement. Click the **Create** icon on the dialog. A new drawing without any predefined shapes will appear.

## User Interface

The following image shows the **Visio 2013** application window.

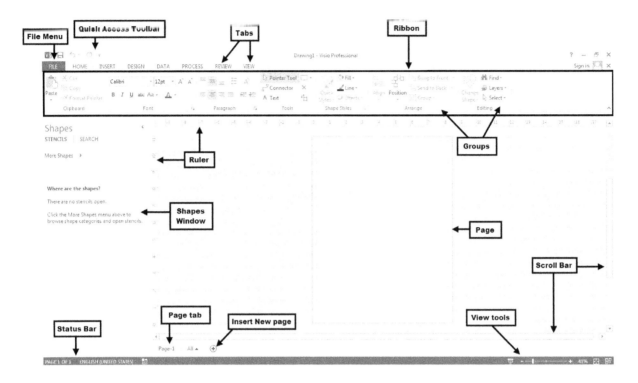

Various components of the user interface are:

## Quick Access Toolbar

The **Quick Access Toolbar** has some commonly used commands such as **New**, **Open**, **Save**, **Undo**, **Redo**, **Regenerate,** and so on. You can add more commands to the **Quick Access Toolbar** by clicking on the down-arrow next to it, and then selecting commands from the drop-down menu. You can also use the **More Commands** option and add new commands from the **Visio Options** dialog.

## File Menu

The **File Menu** appears when you click on the **File** tab located at the top left corner of the window. The **File Menu** has a list of self-explanatory menus. You can start a new file, open an existing file, save, print, share, and export files using the File Menu. Click **Options** on the File Menu to open the **Options** dialog.

The **General** page shows the options related to the user interface, office theme, and personalization.

The **Proofing** page shows the spelling and AutoCorrect options.

The **Save** page shows the options to set the file format, auto recovery settings, and server files location.

The **Language** page shows the options to set the language preferences.

The **Advanced** page shows the editing, display, save/open, and general options. Under the **General** section, check the **Run in developer mode** option to show additional options in the User Interface.

The **Customize Ribbon** page allows you to add or remove commands from the Ribbon.

The **Quick Access Toolbar** page allows you to add or remove commands from the Quick Access Toolbar.

The **Add-Ins** page displays the plug-ins added to Visio. You can manage plug-ins by clicking the **Go** button located at the bottom.

The **Trust Center** page displays the options related to the file security. You can click the **Trust Center Settings** button to define the security settings.

## Ribbon

Ribbon is located at the top of the window. It has various tabs. When you click on a tab, various groups appear. These groups have commands.

Various tabs available on the ribbon are given next.

### HOME tab

The **HOME** tab has commands to create and edit drawings. In addition, it has commands that are most commonly used.

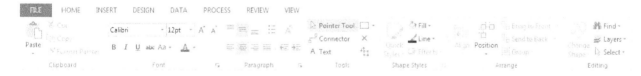

### INSERT tab

This tab has commands to insert objects into the drawing. You can insert new pages using the **Pages** group. The **Illustrations** group allows you to insert pictures, charts, and CAD Drawings. The **Diagram Parts** group allows you to insert containers, callouts, and connectors. You can add Hyperlinks to any shape of the drawing using the **Links** group. The **Text** group helps you to insert text boxes, floating screen tips, other documents and drawings in the form of objects, text fields, and symbols.

# Microsoft Visio 2013 Basics

## DESIGN tab

This tab has commands to modify the page design.

The **Page Setup** group allows you to change the page size and orientation. The page sizes depend on the selected units. The **Auto Size** command changes the page size automatically if the diagram parts overlap the boundaries of the page.  In addition, you can open the **Page Setup** dialog by clicking the arrow located at the bottom right corner.

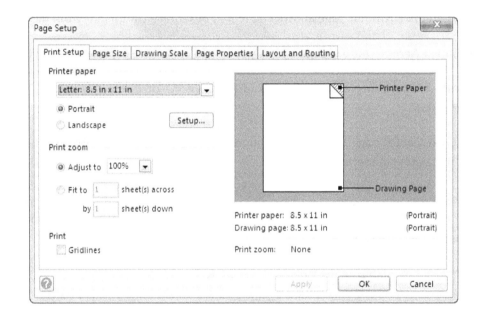

The **Themes** group allows you to apply various color themes to the diagram parts and background.

The **Background** group has options to apply borders, titles, and background to the page.

The **Layout** group has options to change the layout and connector styles of the diagram.

## DATA tab

This tab has commands to connect the drawing to the external database. Note that this tab is available in the Professional and Premium editions. The **External Data** group allows you to attach the external data to the diagram parts. The **Display Data** group allows you to show the data along with the diagram. You can show or hide the Shape Data Window and External Data Window using the **Show/Hide** group.

# Microsoft Visio 2013 Basics

## PROCESS tab

This tab has commands to create a sub process, validate a process, and work with SharePoint. The **Subprocess** group allows you to divide a large diagram into various sub processes. You can select a portion of the large diagram and convert it into a sub process. You can access the sub process by using the hyperlink created on the large diagram. The **Diagram Validation** group allows you check the diagram so that it matches the rules and standards. The Share Point Workflow group allows you to import and export to SharePoint Workflows.

## REVIEW tab

This tab has commands to proofread, translate, add comments, and create shape reports.

## VIEW tab

This tab has commands to zoom, pan, rotate, or change the view mode. You can switch to the Prensentation Mode by using the **Views** group. The **Show** group allows you to show/hide rulers, page breaks, grid, and guide. Also, you can show/hide different types of Task panes. The **Zoom** group has options to maginify the page to various sizes, and fit the page to window size and its width. These commands are also available on the Status bar on the lower right corner of the window. The **Visual Aids** group allows you to toggle the tools that help you to create drawings easily. The **Window** group allows you to switch between windows of multiple drawings. The **Macros** group allows you to create and run macros, and other Add-Ons.

In addition, that are some contextual tabs that appear on the ribbon while perfoming specific operations.

## Collapsing the Ribbon

# Microsoft Visio 2013 Basics

You can increase the drawing page by collapsing the ribbon. To collapse the ribbon, click the upward arrow located at the bottom right corner of the ribbon (or) press Ctrl+F1.

To expand the ribbon, double-click on anyone of its tabs.

## Status bar

This is available below the page. It shows the status while using the commands. You can also record macros from the status bar.

## Shapes Window

It contains a list of stencils that can be used to create a drawing. A stencil in real world is a perforated plastic material with various kinds of shapes. Similarly, a stencil in Visio is a collection of predefined shapes that can be dragged into the page. Shapes are available in the Shapes Window in all the templates of Visio except the Blank template. The shapes in the Shapes Window vary based on the type of template that you choose. For example, the Floor Plan template has shapes to create architectural floor plan, whereas the Organization Chart template has shapes to create an organizational chart.

In addition to the existing shapes, you can load more shapes in the Shapes Window by clicking **More Shapes** and selecting the required stencil.

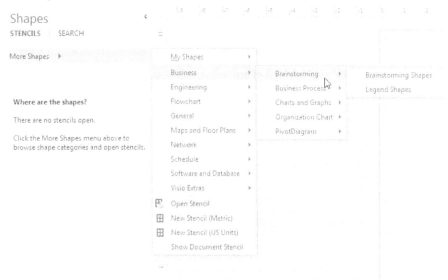

On the Shapes Window, click the different stencils and notice the shapes listed. In addition, you can search for the required shape by clicking the SEARCH option and typing the keyword in the SEARCH BAR. You can click the arrow located on the top right corner of the Shapes Window to minimize/maximize its size.

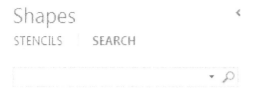

By default, the stencil is docked in the Shapes Window. You can undock a stencil by right clicking on it and selecting Float Window. You can drag the stencil to a desired location. If you want to remove a stencil from the Shapes Window, right click on it and select **Close**.

## Presentation Mode

The Presentation Mode helps you to see only the diagram. To activate this mode, click **View > Views > Presentation Mode** on the ribbon (or) click the **Presentation Mode** icon at the bottom of the window. Press F5 to return back to the editing mode.

## Ruler, Grid, Page Breaks, and Guides

Ruler, Grid, Page Breaks, and Guides are the visual aids which help you to create diagrams easily. The Ruler is displayed above and left side of the drawing page. You can hide the Ruler by unchecking the **Ruler** option on the Show group of the VIEW ribbon tab.

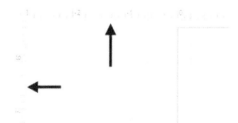

The Grid helps you to position the diagram parts precisely. However, the grid is not displayed by default. Check the **Grid** option on the **Show** group of the **VIEW** ribbon tab to display the grid.

The Page Break is the border on the drawing page enclosing the printable area. The Page Break is also displayed when you position a shape on the edge of the drawing page. You can hide the Page Break by unchecking the **Page Break** option on the **Show** group of the **VIEW** ribbon tab.

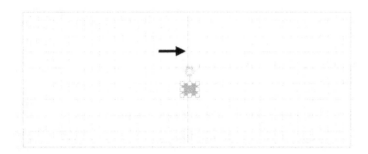

Guides help you to align the diagram parts. You can create guides on the drawing page by clicking on the Ruler and dragging it. However, you can hide the guides by unchecking the **Guide** option on the **Show** group of the **VIEW** ribbon tab.

# Task Panes

You can show or hide various window panes by using the **Task Pane** drop-down.

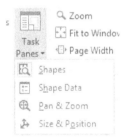

# Visual Aids

The visual aids help you to position and connect diagram parts easily. The three major visual aids are **Dynamic Grid**, **AutoConnect**, and **Connection Points**.

The **Dynamic Grid** helps you to position a shape with respect to an already existing one. When you drag a shape from the Shapes Window and move the pointer near an already existing shape, the dotted lines appear helping you to align the shape horizontally or vertically with respect to an existing shape. However, you can hide these dotted lines by unchecking the **Dynamic Grid** option on the **Visual Aids** group of the **VIEW** ribbon tab.

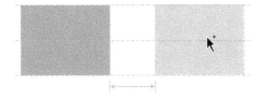

The **AutoConnect** option helps you to connect a new shape to an existing one, automatically. Place the pointer on a shape and notice the four blue arrows pointing outwards. You can click on these blue arrows and connect a new shape to an existing one. However, you can hide these arrows by unchecking the **AutoConnect** option on the **Visual Aids** group of the **VIEW** ribbon tab.

The **Connection Point** option displays connection points when you move a connector near a shape. You can turn off the Connection Points by unchecking the **Connection Point** option on the **Visual Aids** group of the **VIEW** ribbon tab.

# Multiple Windows

Visio allows you to open multiple documents at a time and navigate between them. The commands available on the **Window** group of the **VIEW** ribbon tab. The **New Window** command allows you to open a new window of the existing document. The **Arrange All** command displays all the documents by arranging them in vertical or horizontal manner. The **Cascade** command arranges one window over the other. The **Switch Windows** drop-down allows you to switch between different windows.

# Mouse Functions

Various functions of the mouse buttons are:

## Left Mouse button (MB1)

When you double-click the left mouse button (MB1) on a shape, the text box would appear. You can edit the text of the shape.

## Right Mouse button (MB3)

Select an object and click this button to open the shortcut menu related to it.

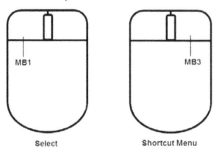

## Middle Mouse button (MB2)

Press the middle mouse and drag the mouse to pan the view.

MB2+Drag

Pan

# Tutorial 1 (Creating Basic Flow Charts)

## Starting a new Basic Flow Chart

1. Start Visio 2013.
2. On the Backstage, click the **Flowchart** category.

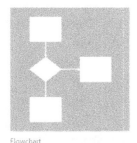

Flowchart

3. Click the **Basic Flowchart** template.
4. Select **US Units** and click **Create**. A new Visio file is created using the **Basic Flowchart** template.

## Adding Shapes

1. On the Shapes Window, click the **Basic Flowchart Shapes** stencil.
2. Click on the **Start/End** shape.

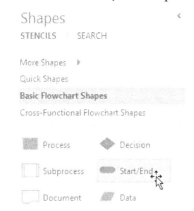

3. Hold the left mouse button and drag the shape into the drawing page.

4. Release the left mouse button and notice that the shape is selected, automatically. Also, notice the resize and rotate handles on the selected shape.
5. On the Shapes Window, select the **Decision** shape and drag it into the drawing page.
6. Place the left mouse button below the Start/End shape and notice the visual aids. They help you to position the shape with respect to the already existing shape.

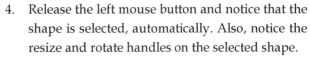

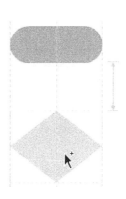

7. Release the left mouse button to position the **Decision** shape.
8. Click the **DEVELOPER** tab on the ribbon. Follow the next two steps if the **DEVELOPER** tab is not visible.
9. Click the **FILE** tab on the ribbon and click **Options** on the File menu.
10. On the **Visio Options** dialog, click the **Advanced** tab and check the **Run in developer mode** option. Click **OK**.
11. On the **DEVELOPER** tab, on the **Show/Hide** group, check the **Document Stencil** option. Notice the **Document** Stencil on the Shapes Window. The two shapes that you placed on the drawing page are copied into the Document Stencil. Also, they become a part of the current drawing. You can modify these shapes without effecting the original ones.

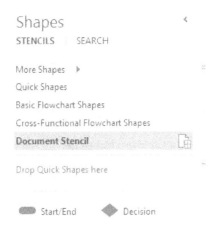

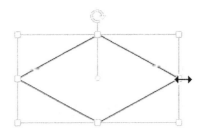

12. Press and hold the Ctrl key and place the pointer on the Decision shape. Notice the plus symbol next to the pointer.
13. Hold the Ctrl key and drag the Decision symbol. A copy of the Decision symbol is attached to the pointer.
14. Position the copy on the lower left-side.

18. Close the window. **The Update 'Decision' and all of its instances** message appears.

19. Click **Yes** and notice that all the instances of the **Decision** shape are updated.

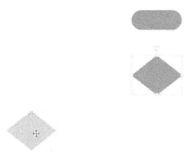

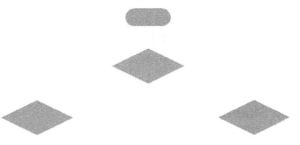

15. Likewise, place another copy of the Decision shape on the lower right-side.

20. On the **DEVELOPER** tab, uncheck the **Document Stencil** option.

## Adding Connected Shapes

1. Place the pointer on the lower left Decision shape and notice the four arrows pointing outwards.
2. Place the pointer on the downward arrow and notice a palette with four shapes. You can add anyone of these shapes to the already existing shapes

16. On the **Document** Stencil, right click on the **Decision** shape and select **Edit Master > Edit Master Shape**. The **Decision** shape appears in a separate window.
17. Select the shape and stretch it horizontally.

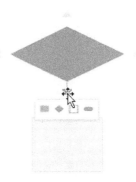

Also, notice that the top four shapes in the Shapes window are displayed on the palette. You can select the shapes to be displayed on the palette.

3. On the Shapes Window, click and drag the Custom 4 shape into the top portion of the stencil.

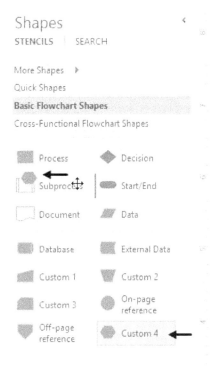

4. Place the pointer on the lower left Decision shape and on the down arrow. Notice the Custom 4 shape displayed on the palette.

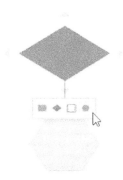

5. Click the **Decision** shape on the palette. A new **Decision** shape is added. Also, a connection is created between the existing the shapes.

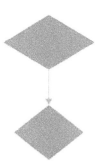

## Changing Shapes

1. Click the new Decision shape.
2. On the ribbon, click **HOME > Editing > Change Shape** drop-down. Notice the different shapes available on the drop-down.
3. Place the pointer on each of the shapes and notice that the preview changes.

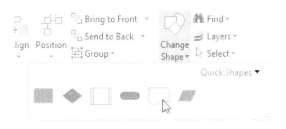

4. On the **Change Shapes** drop-down, click on the down arrow located at the top right corner.
5. Select the **Basic Flowchart Shapes** stencil from the drop-down and notice the new shapes.

6. Add other shapes to the diagram, as shown.

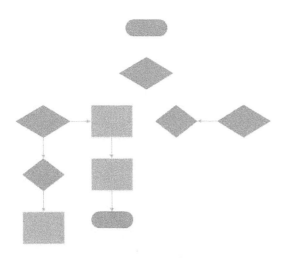

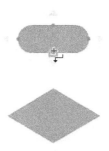

7. On the Shapes Window, click the **Process** shape and drag it onto the drawing page.
8. Release the pointer on the line connecting the **Process** shape and **Start/End** shape. The shape is added between the two existing shapes. Also, the equal distance is maintained between the shapes.

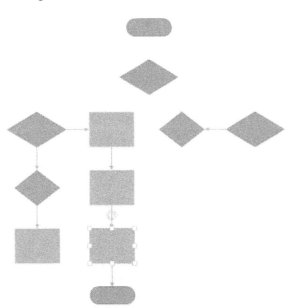

## Creating Connectors

1. On the ribbon, click **HOME > Tools > Connector** .
2. Zoom to the top portion of the diagram.
3. Select the Connector point of the **Start/End** shape, as shown.

4. Press and hold the left mouse button and drag the pointer.
5. Select the connector point of the Decision shape, as shown. A connector is created between the two shapes.

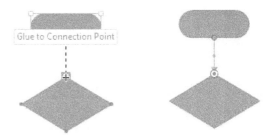

6. Likewise, create connectors, as shown.

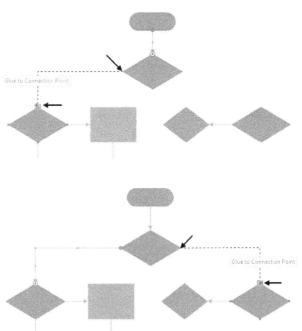

7. On the ribbon, on the **Tools** group, click the **Pointer Tool** icon.

## Moving the Shapes

1. On the ribbon, on the **Tools** group, click the

**Pointer Tool** icon.

2. Select the Decision shape, as shown.
3. Drag and position it, as shown. The connector connected to it is modified.

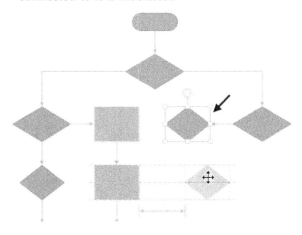

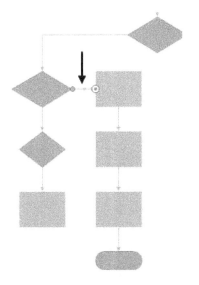

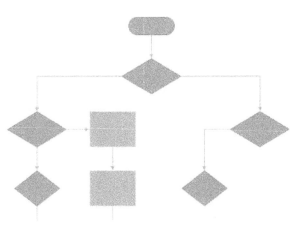

4. Select the horizontal connector between the **Decision** and **Process** shapes.
5. Press **Delete** to remove it.

6. Drag a selection window across the **Process** and **Start/End** shapes.

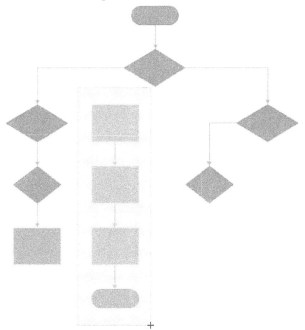

7. Click on anyone of the selected shapes and drag the pointer downward.
8. Release the pointer and notice that the four shapes are moved. Also, a new page is added as the diagram size increases.

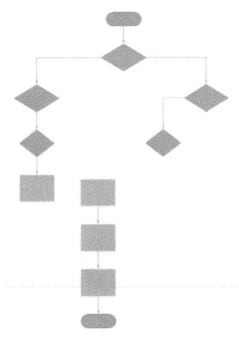

☑ Dynamic Grid
☑ AutoConnect
☑ Connection Points     w
Visual Aids

2. On the **Snap & Glue** dialog, click the **Advanced** tab.
3. Under the **Shape extension options** section, check the **Horz line at endpoint** option, and then click **OK**.
4. On the ribbon, on the **Tools** group, click the **Connection Point** ✕ icon.
5. Zoom to the connector between the **Decision** and **Process** shape.
6. Press the Ctrl key and select the connector.
7. Press the Ctrl key and place the pointer on the Connection point of the Decision shape. The horizontal extension line appears from the connection point.
8. Move the pointer on the extension line.
9. Click at the intersection point between the extension line and connector.

8. On the ribbon, click **HOME > Tools > Connector** ⬡ .
9. Create the connector between the Process and Decision shape.

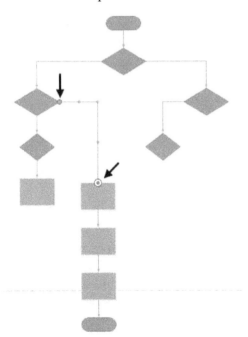

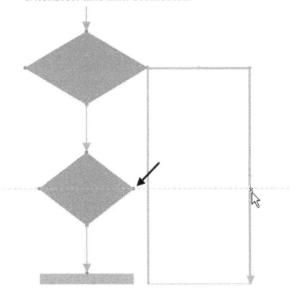

A connection point is created on the connector.

## Adding Connection Points

1. On the **VIEW** tab of the ribbon, click the down arrow on the **Visual Aids** group.

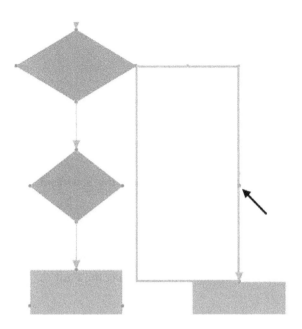

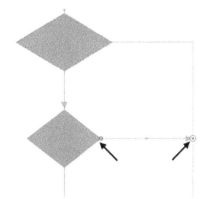

10. Press the Ctrl key and click on the connector between the **Process** and **Start/End** shape at the bottom.

13. Create the connector between the Decision shape located at the right side and the vertical connector, as shown.

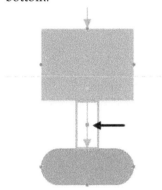

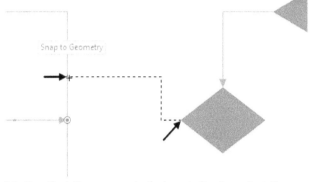

Notice that the green circle is not displayed at the intersection of the two connectors, which means that they are not connected.

11. On the ribbon, click **HOME > Tools > Connector** .

12. Create a connector between the **Decision** and **Connection Point**. Notice a green circle at the intersection between the two connectors. It indicates that the two connectors are connected together.

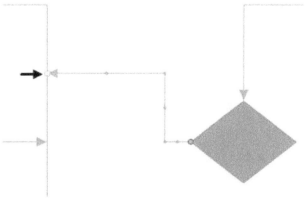

14. Click and drag the end point of the connector and release it on the Connection Point.

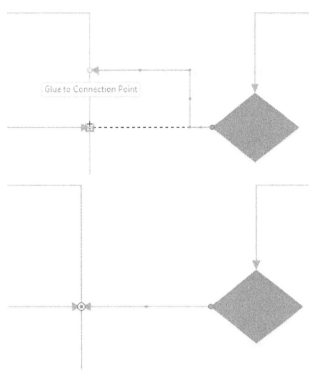

15. Create other Connection Points and connectors, as shown.

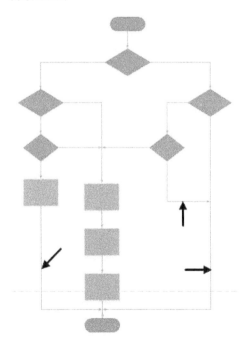

## Adding Text

1. Click on the **Start/End** shape located at the top.
2. Type **Start**.

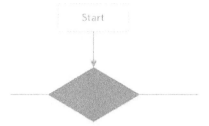

3. Click on the **Decision** shape below the **Start/End** shape.
4. Type **Quality Score?**.
5. Likewise, add text to other shapes.
6. Press Ctrl+A to select all the texts.
7. On the ribbon, on the **Font** group, set the **Font Size** to 12 pt.

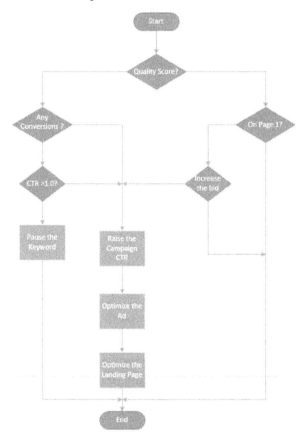

8. Select the left connector of the 'Quality Score?' decision.
9. Type **Poor**.

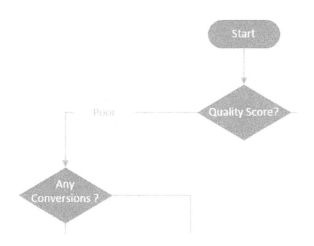

10. Likewise, add text to other connectors, as shown.

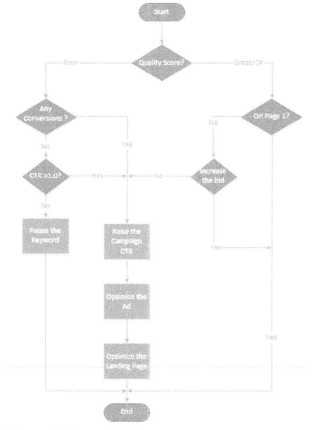

## Shape Fill options

1. On the ribbon, click **DESIGN > Themes > No Theme**.

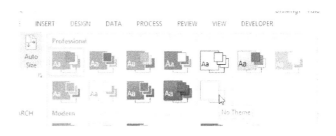

2. Press Ctrl+A to select all the shapes available in the diagram.
3. On the ribbon, click **HOME > Shape Styles > Fill drop-down**.
4. Place the pointer on various colors on the **Fill** drop-down and notice the preview on the drawing page.

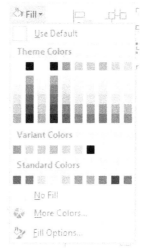

You can use various Theme Colors, which are already available in the predefined themes. The Variant Colors are different type colors that are applied within a selected theme. Also, there are some Standard Colors available on the Fill drop-down.

5. Click the **More Colors** option on the **Fill** drop-down. The **Colors** dialog appears showing different Standard Colors in a hexagonal format.

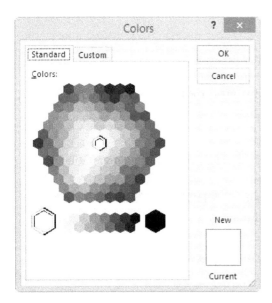

6. Click the **Custom** tab on the **Colors** dialog.
7. Drag down the arrow located on the right side and notice the Red, Green, Blue values change.
8. Drag the pointer in the Colors section to select a custom color. You can also type-in the Red, Green, and Blue values to specify a color. You can find various colors with RGB values on the internet (or) use a standard chart available in your organization to enter the RGB values.
9. Set **Color Model** to **HSL** to specify the color by adjusting the Hue, Saturation, and Luminosity.
10. Click **Cancel** on the **Colors** dialog.
11. On the ribbon, click **HOME > Shape Styles > Fill** drop-down, and click the **Fill Options** option located at the bottom. The **Format Shape** pane appears on the right side of the window. You can select the **No Fill**, **Solid Fill**, **Gradient Fill**, or **Pattern Fill** option
12. Select the **Gradient Fill** option.

You can select predefined gradients from the **Preset gradients** drop-down.

Use the **Type** drop-down to specify the gradient type.

Use the **Direction** or **Angle** drop-downs to specify the gradient direction.

Use the gradient slider or **Position** box to change the Gradient percentage. You can add or remove stops from the gradient slider using the **Add gradient stop** 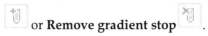 or **Remove gradient stop** .

Use the **Color** drop-down to adjust the gradient color. You can also select the stops on the gradient slider and set their color.

Use the **Transparency** and **Brightness** sliders to adjust the transparency and brightness. You can select the gradient stops and adjust their transparency and brightness.

Keep the **Rotate with shape** option checked, if you want to rotate the gradient along with the shape.

13. Select the **Pattern Fill** option.

Use the **Pattern** drop-down to set the pattern type.

Use the **Foreground** and **Transparency** options to the set the pattern color and transparency.

## Applying Effects to Shapes

1. Select any shape from the diagram.
2. On the ribbon, click **HOME > Shape Styles > Effects** drop-down. Notice the sub menus available on the drop-down.

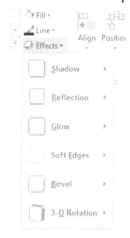

3. Click on the **SHADOW** submenu and select any predefined Shadow type.
4. Click the **Shadow Options** option located at the bottom of the **SHADOW** submenu to open the **Format Shape** pane.

Use the **Color** drop-down to change the shadow color.

Drag the **Transparency**, **Size**, **Blur**, **Angle**, and **Distance** sliders to change their values.

5. Expand the **REFLECTION** section.

Use the **Preset** drop-down to select the predefined reflection type.

6. Examine the other effects and close the **Format Shape** pane.

## Formatting Lines

1. Select any shape from the diagram.
2. On the ribbon, click **HOME > Shape Styles > Line drop-down**.
3. Place the pointer on various colors on the **Line** drop-down and notice the preview on the drawing page.

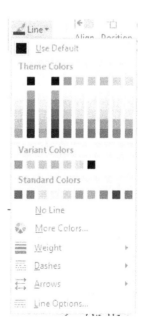

Use the **Weight** submenu to change the line weight of the shape boundary.

Use the **Dashes** submenu to change the line type.

Use the **Arrows** submenu to add arrows at ends of the lines. The arrows can be added to the connectors.

4. Click the **Line Options** option at the bottom of the **Line** drop-down. The **Format Shape** pane appears.

On the **Format Shape** pane, you can select three different types of line fills: No File, Solid Fill, and Gradient Fill.

5. Examine the other settings on the **Format Shapes** pane and close it.

## Formatting Texts

1. On ribbon, **HOME > Tools > Text** $^A$ .
2. Click on the drawing page and type **Sample text**.
3. Zoom into the text area.

Sample Text

4. Click the **Pointer Tool** icon on the **Tools** group of the ribbon.

5. Place the pointer on the text and notice the arrows around it. The text is a rectangular shape without any fill and boundary.

6. Double-click on the text and notice that the complete text selected.
7. Click anywhere in the text and add new text to it.

8. Double-click on the text to select it.

On the ribbon, the **Font** group has options to change the Font, Font Size, Font Style (Regular, Italic, Underline, Bold, and Strikethrough), Case, and Font Color.

The **Paragraph** group has options to align the text block, align the text, add bullets to it, adjust the indent, and rotate the text.

9. Click the arrow located at the bottom right corner of the **Fonts** group. The **Text** dialog appears and it has some additional options such as **Position**, **Language**, and **Transparency**.

The **Character** tab on the **Text** dialog has the **Scaling** and **Spacing** drop-downs. The **Scaling** drop-down is used to narrow or stretch the font. The **Spacing** drop-down is used to increase or decrease the spacing between the letters. For example, select the **Expanded** option and set the spacing in the **By** box. Click **Apply** to increase the spacing between letters.

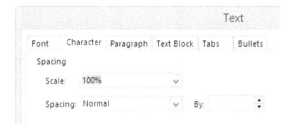

The **Paragraph** tab on the **Text** dialog has the **Alignment** options to align the text within the box. In addition to that, you can specify the line **Indentation** and **Spacing** between the lines by entering specific values.

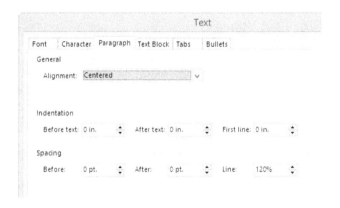

The **Text Block** tab on the **Text** dialog has the options to align the text block (Top, Middle, and Bottom). In addition, you can add margins spaces around the text and set a background color for the text.

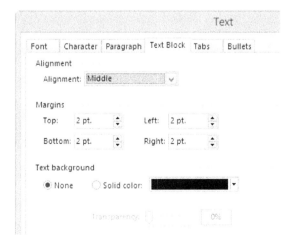

The **Tabs** tab has options to add new a tab spacing. The default tab spacing is 0.5 in.

The **Bullets** tab has options to apply various types of bullets to the text. You specify the bullet size and position. In addition, you can use a custom symbol/text as bullet by entering it in the **Bullet characters** box.

10. Close the **Text** dialog.
11. On the Shapes Window, select and drag the **Process** shape onto the drawing page.
12. Type-in "Sample Text".

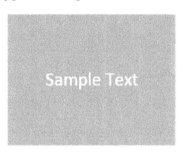

13. On the ribbon, click **HOME > Tools > Text Block**, and select the text.
14. Click the Rotate text handle and rotate the text. Notice that only the text is rotated. You can change the position of the text independently.

15. Click the **Pointer Tool** icon on the **Tools** group.
16. Click and drag the **Process** shape and notice that the text also moves along with the shape.

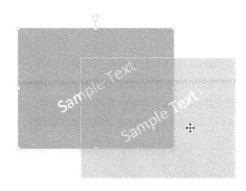

# Tutorial 2 (Inserting Objects)

You can insert Illustrations into a Visio diagram using the commands available on the **Illustrations** group of the **INSERT** ribbon tab.

## Inserting Pictures

1. Start a new Visio drawing using anyone of the templates.
2. Click the **Pictures** icon on the **Illustrations** tab to insert pictures from your local hard drive. You can also use the **Online Pictures** command to insert image from the internet.
3. Go to the location of the image file and double-click on it. The image is inserted on the drawing page. Also, the **PICTURE TOOLS FORMAT** tab appears. On this tab, you can adjust the Brightness and Contrast of the image or use **AutoBalance** command to do it, automatically. You can also compress the picture, set the border style, move it front or backward on the drawing page, rotate, and crop it.
4. Use the handles located on the image to rotate or resize it.

## Inserting Charts

1. Open an Excel file and copy as chart.
2. Switch to the Visio document and paste the chart.

## Inserting CAD Drawings

1. On the ribbon, click **INSERT > Illustrations > CAD Drawing**.
2. Go to the location of the image file and double-click on it.

## Adding Callouts

1. Drag a shape into the drawing page.
2. Select the shape from the diagram and click **INSERT > Diagram Parts > Callouts** .
3. Select the callout style from the Callout gallery to add it to the shape.
4. Type-in the callout text and click anywhere on the drawing page.

## Adding Text Boxes

1. On the ribbon, click **INSERT > Text > Text Box > Horizontal Text Box**.
2. Drag a rectangular box on the drawing page and type-in the text.

Sample Text

3. On the ribbon, click **INSERT > Text > Text Box > Vertical Text Box**.
4. Drag a vertical rectangular box and type-in the text.

## Adding ScreenTips

1. Drag a shape on to the drawing page.
2. Select a shape from the diagram and click **INSERT > Text > ScreenTip**.

3. Type-in the text in the **Shape ScreenTip** dialog and click **OK**.
4. Place pointer on the shape and notice the screen tip.

## Adding Fields

1. Select a shape from the diagram and click

    **INSERT > Text > Field** ▭.
2. Select the field category from the **Category** list.
3. Select the **Field** name and click **OK**.

## Adding Symbols

1. Double-click on the shape to activate the text mode.
2. On the ribbon, click **INSERT > Text > Symbol**

    Ω and select a symbol.
3. On the **Symbol** drop-down click the **More Symbols** option to open the **Symbol** dialog.
4. On the **Symbol** dialog, click the **Symbol** tab and set the Font type. The symbols under the selected font appear. You can filter symbols by selecting a **Subset**.
5. Click the **Special Characters** tab to select different special characters.
6. Select the required symbol or special character and click **Insert**.
7. Close the dialog after inserting the symbols.

## Tutorial 2 (Validating Diagrams)

Visio allows you to check the diagram so that it follows all the rules. By default, the rules are define as per the selected template.

1. Download the Tutorial 3 file and open it.
2. On the ribbon, click **PROCESS > Diagram**

    **Validation > Check Diagram** ▭. Visio checks the diagram and displays the issues in the diagram.
3. On the Issues window, click the issues one-by-one view them in the diagram.

| Rule | Category |
|---|---|
| Connected shape is not recognized as a Flowchart shape. | Connectivity |
| Connected shape is not recognized as a Flowchart shape. | Connectivity |
| Connected shape is not recognized as a Flowchart shape. | Connectivity |
| Connected shape is not recognized as a Flowchart shape. | Connectivity |
| Connected shape is not recognized as a Flowchart shape. | Connectivity |
| Connected shape is not recognized as a Flowchart shape. | Connectivity |
| Connected shape is not recognized as a Flowchart shape. | Connectivity |
| Connector is not glued at both ends. | Connectivity |
| Connector is not glued at both ends. | Connectivity |
| Connector is not glued at both ends. | Connectivity |
| Connector is not glued at both ends. | Connectivity |

You can ignore an issue by right clicking on it and selecting **Ignore This Issue**. You can also ignore a rule by selecting the **Ignore Rule** option.

4. Uncheck the **Issues Window** option on the **Diagram Validation** group of the **PROCESS** ribbon tab.

## Tutorial 3 (Applying Themes to Diagrams)

A theme is a set of colors, fonts, effects, styles, and embellishments applied to a diagram to make it look attractive. By default, the **Office** theme applied to a diagram. However, you apply a different theme as per your requirement.

1. Download the Tutorial 4 file and open it.
2. On the ribbon, click **DESIGN** tab and place the pointer on different themes available on the **Themes** group. The look of the diagram changes.
3. Click on the drop-down to display the **Themes** gallery with different theme categories.

4. Click on the **Ion** theme under the **Professional** category.

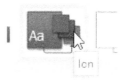

Now, the selected theme will be applied to any new shapes that you add to the diagram. If you do not want this to happen, then deselect the **Apply Theme to New Shapes** option on the **Themes** gallery.

5. Place the pointer on different variants available on the **Variants** group. Different variations of a same theme are displayed.
6. Click on the drop-down to view more variations such as Colors, Effects, Connectors, and Embellishments.

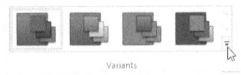

Variants

7. Click on the **Colors** drop-down and notice the different color variations.
8. Click on the **Effects** drop-down and place the pointer on different effects.
9. Click on the **Connectors** drop-down and notice the connector types related different themes.
10. Click on the **Embellishments** drop-down and select the **High** option. More effects are added to the shape.
11. Likewise, select the **Medium, Low, Automatic** options and see the difference.

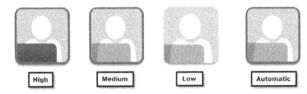

## Background
1. To change the background of the drawing page, click **DESIGN > Backgrounds > Backgrounds** and select a background style. You can also select a background color by clicking the **Background color** drop-down on the Background gallery.

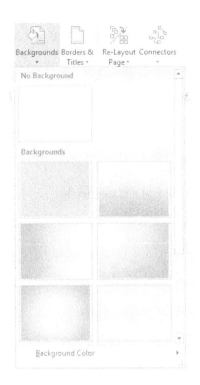

2. Notice the **VBackground-1** tab at the bottom of the drawing page. Click the **VBackground-1** tab and add text or logo to the background. It will be reflected on the foreground.

## Borders and Titles
1. On the ribbon, click **DESIGN > Backgrounds > Borders & Titles** and select a border & title. The border, title, date, and page number are applied to the sheet.
2. Click the **VBackground-1** tab below the drawing page and double click on the Title to edit it.

## Creating New Theme Colors
1. On the ribbon, click **DESIGN > Variants > More > Colors > Create New Theme Colors**.
2. On the **New Theme Colors** dialog, type-in Sample in the **Name** box.
3. Change the **Theme Color** Accents and notice the difference in the preview section of the dialog.
4. Click **Apply** to preview the theme on the drawing page. If the resultant theme is not as desired, then make changes on the dialog and click **Apply**.
5. Click **OK** to close the dialog.

6. On the ribbon, click **DESIGN > Variants > More > Colors** and notice the **Sample** theme color under the **Custom** section.
7. Right click on **Sample** theme color and select **Edit**, **Duplicate**, or **Delete** option.

# Tutorial 4 (Publishing your Diagrams)

You can publish your diagrams in various ways such as printing, exporting to other formats, and saving to cloud.

## Printing Diagrams

1. Download the Tutorial 5 file and open it.
2. Click **File > Print**. The **Print** options appear on the Backstage.

3. Select a printer from the **Printer** drop-down. You can also add a printer by selecting the **Add Printer** option on the **Printer** drop-down.
4. Select an option from the **Settings** drop-down. You can choose to print all pages, print the current page, specify the range of pages to print, print a selection of a diagram, and print the current view.
5. Select the **No Background** option on the **Settings** drop-down if you want to hide the background.
6. Select the orientation of the drawing page from the **Orientation** drop-down.
7. Select the sheet size from the **Size** drop-down.
8. Select the **Color** or **Black and white** option from the **Color** drop-down. You can add the **Greyscale** option to this drop-down by clicking the **Printer Properties** option and selecting the **Black & White** option from the **Paper/Quality** tab.
9. Click the **Page Setup** option to view advanced print options.
10. On the **Page Setup** dialog, specify the Print Setup, Page Size, Drawing Scale, Page Properties, and Layout and Routing settings, and then click **OK**.
11. Click the **Print** button to print the drawing.

# Tutorial 5 (Creating Brainstorming Diagrams)

1. Start Visio 2013.
2. On the Backstage, click the **Business** category and select the **Brainstorming Diagram** template.

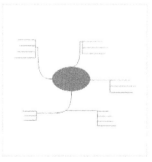

Brainstorming Diagram

3. Select the **US Units** and click **Create**. The drawing page appears along with the **Outline Window**.
4. On the Shapes Window, click the **Brainstorming Shapes** stencil.
5. Drag the **Main topic** shape and place it on the center portion of the drawing page.

6. Type **Marketing Plan** and click anywhere on the drawing page. The tope node of the diagram appears on the Outline Window.

Also, notice the **BRAINSTORMING** tab on the ribbon.

7. Select the main topic shape
8. On the **BRAINSTORMING** tab, click **Add Topics > Subtopic** (or) right click on the main topic and select **Add subtopic**.
9. Type **Product** and click anywhere on the drawing page.

10. Select the Main topic shape and click **Multiple Subtopics** on the **BRAINSTORMING** tab

(or) right click on the Main topic and select **Add Multiple Subtopics**.
11. On the **Add Multiple Topics** dialog, type Price and press Enter.
12. Likewise, type other topics, and click OK.

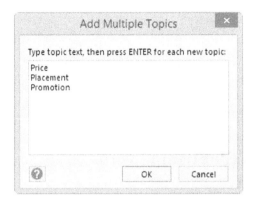

13. Select the main topic and drag it downward.

14. Select the Promotion subtopic and click the **Multiple Subtopics** icon on the BRAINSTORMING.
15. On the **Add Multiple Topics** dialog, type Trade Shows and press Enter.
16. Type Mailings and click **OK**.

17. On the Outline Window, right click on the **Price** node and select **Add subtopic**.
18. Select the New Topic node, type **Advertising**, and press Enter.

# Microsoft Visio 2013 Basics

In a marketing plan, Advertising will not come under Price. You need to bring Advertising under Promotion

19. On the Outline Window, click and drag the **Advertising** node and release it on the Promotion node. The Advertising node becomes the part of Promotion.

20. Select the **Trade shows** subtopic and click **BRAINSTORMING > Arrange > Change Topic**.

21. Select **Rectangle** from the **Change Shape** dialog and click **OK**.

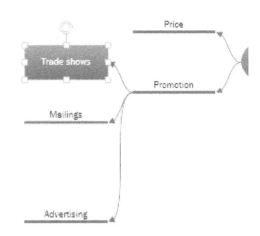

22. Press the Ctrl key and select the **Mailings** and **Advertising** shapes.

23. Right click on anyone of the selected shapes and select **Change Topic** Shape.

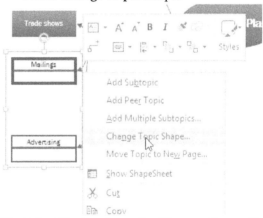

24. Select **Rectangle** on the **Change Shape** dialog and click **OK**.

25. Click and move the **Advertising** shape up.

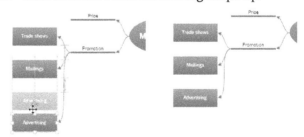

26. On the **BRAINSTORMING** tab, click **Manage > Diagram Style**.

27. On the **Brainstorming Style** dialog, examine the different types of styles.

28. Select the **Boxy** style and click **OK**. The diagram style is changed to **Boxy**.

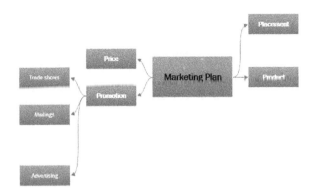

29. On the **BRAINSTORMING** tab, click **Arrange > Layout** .

30. Examine the different **Layouts** and **Connector** types on the **Layout** dialog.

31. Select the **Top to Bottom** layout and **Straight** connector.

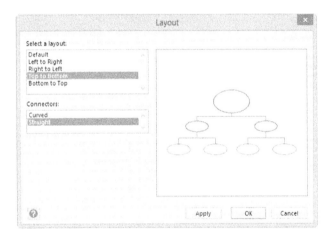

32. Click **OK**.

33. On the **DESIGN** tab of the ribbon, click **Themes > No Theme**.

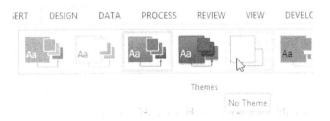

Notice that different colors are applied for each hierarchy.

34. On the **BRAINSTORMING** tab, click **Manage > Export Data > To Microsoft Word**.

Note that the **Export Data** options are available only when a compatible version of Microsoft Word or Excel available. For example, if you have Visio 2013, then you need to have Word 2013 to export the diagram to a Word document.

35. Specify the location of the XML file and click Save. The diagram is exported to the XML format and opened in Microsoft Word.

Notice that the Main topic is designated as Heading 1 and subtopics as Heading 2. The topics under each subtopics are designated as Heading 3.

**Marketing Plan**

*Product*

*Price*

*Placement*

*Promotion*

Trade shows

Mailings

Advertising

You can use this data to create diagrams and charts in Word.

36. Close the Word document.

37. On the **BRAINSTORMING** tab, click **Manage > Export Data > To Microsoft Excel**.
38. Specify the location of the XML file and click **Save**. The XML file is opened in Microsoft Excel.

Notice that the Main topic is designated as T1 and subtopics as T1.1, T1.2, T1.3, and T1.4. The topics under T1.4 are designated as T1.4.1, T1.4.2, and T1.4.3.

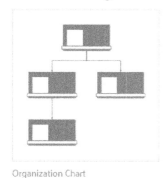

|   | A | B | C |
|---|---|---|---|
| 1 | T1 | Marketing Plan | |
| 2 | T1.1 | Product | |
| 3 | T1.2 | Price | |
| 4 | T1.3 | Placement | |
| 5 | T1.4 | Promotion | |
| 6 | T1.4.1 | Trade shows | |
| 7 | T1.4.2 | Mailings | |
| 8 | T1.4.3 | Advertising | |
| 9 | | | |

You can also export the diagram to the XML format directly.

If you want to create a Brainstorming diagram from an Excel or Word document, then convert it into an XML file and use the Import command available on the BRAINSTORMING tab of the ribbon.

# Tutorial 6 (Creating Organizational Charts)

1. Start Visio 2013.
2. On the Backstage, click the **Business** Category and select the **Organizational Chart** template.

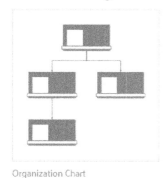

Organization Chart

3. Select the **US Units** and click **Create**.
4. On the Shapes Window, click the **Belt-Organizational Chart Shapes** stencil. You will

notice the different belts such as Executive Belt, Manager Belt, Position Belt, Assistant Belt, and so on, on the shapes window.

You can change the style of the shapes displayed on the Shapes Window by using the **Shapes** group on the **ORG CHART** tab of the ribbon. There are different types of the styles available on the **Shapes** group. Click on stencil to display it on the Shapes Window.

5. Drag the **Executive Belt** shape and place it on the top center portion of the drawing page.

6. On the Shapes Window, click the **Manager Belt**, drag it, and release it on the **Executive Belt**. It will placed under the **Executive belt**.

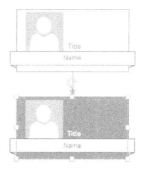

7. Likewise, place three more Manager Belts under the Executive belt.

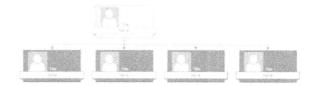

8. Click and drag the extreme right Manager belt, and place it on the extreme left.

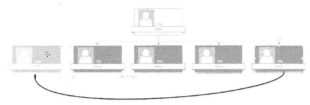

9. On the Shapes Window, click the **Assistant Belt**, drag it, and release it on the Executive Belt. It will placed under the Executive belt.

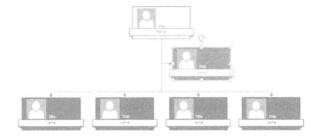

10. Drag the **Position Belt** and drop it on the extreme left **Manager Belt**.
11. Likewise, drop three more instances of the **Position Belt** on the extreme left **Manager Belt**.

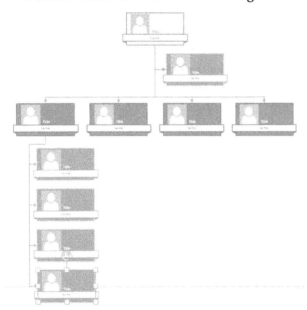

12. On the **ORG CHART** tab of the ribbon, click **Layout > Layout** drop-down. Notice the different types of layouts available in Layout drop-down.

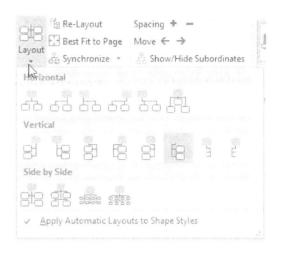

You can select a layout that is suitable to your requirement.

13. Select the extreme left **Manager belt** and click the **Move Right/Down** icon on the **Arrange** group. The Manager belt is moved to right.

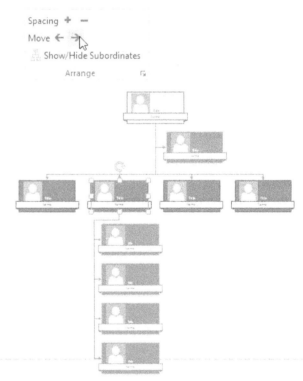

14. Click the top most position under the Manager Belt.
15. On the ribbon, click **DATA > Show/Hide > Shape Data Window**.

16. On the Shape Data Window, enter **Rob** in the **Name** field.

17. Click on the lower most Position belt and enter Bruce in the **Name** field.

18. Select the lower most Position belt and click **ORG CHART > Arrange > Move Left/Up** thrice.

The lower most shape is moved to top.

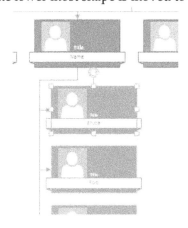

19. Drag and drop the Consultant Belt on the extreme left Manager belt.

20. Drag the Consultant Belt to position it properly.

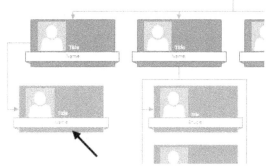

21. Drag and drop the Vacancy Belt on the Consultant Belt.

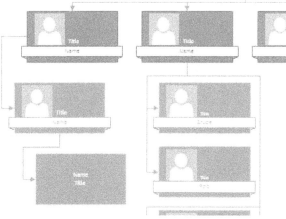

22. Drag the Staff Belt from the Shapes Window and drop it on the lower most Position Belt.

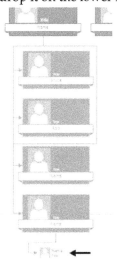

23. Drag the Team Frame shape from the Shapes Window and drop it, as shown.

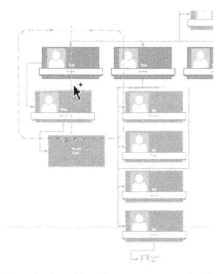

24. Use the handles that appear on the frame to increase its size.

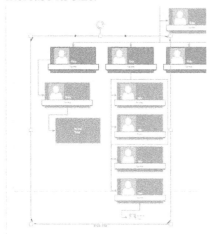

You can enter the team name by clicking on the Team Title located at the bottom.

25. Drag the **Dotted Line Report** shape into the drawing page.
26. Drag the top end point of the dotted line and glue it to the connection point of the second right Manager belt.

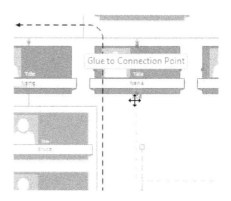

27. Drag the arrow of the dotted line and glue it to the connection point of the Bruce position belt.

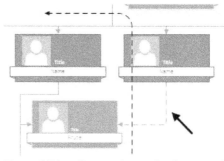

The Dotted Line Report is used when a subordinate reports to more than one manager.

28. Drag the Three positions shape and drop it on the second right Manager Belt. The three positions are placed under the Manager Belt.

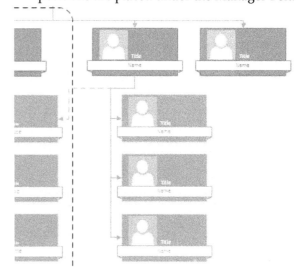

29. Press the Ctrl key and select the three position shapes, and press delete.

30. Drag the **Multiple shapes** shape and drop it on the second right Manager Belt.
31. On the **Add Multiple Shapes** dialog, set the **Number of shapes** to 2, select **Position** from the **Shape** list, and click **OK**.

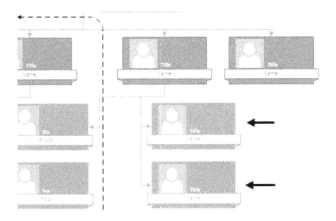

37. On the ribbon, click **ORG CHART > Layout > Best Fit to Page** .
38. Adjust the position and size of the Team frame.

32. Zoom into the top portion of the diagram and select Executive belt shape.
33. On the ribbon, click **ORG CHART > Picture > Insert > Picture** (or) right-click on the shape and select **Insert > Picture**.

34. Go to the location of the picture and double-click on it.

You can use the options on the **Picture** group to change, delete, show or hide the picture.

35. Select the Executive Belt shape located at the top of the chart.
36. On the ribbon, click **ORG CHART > Shapes > Notch**. The chart style is changed to Notch type.

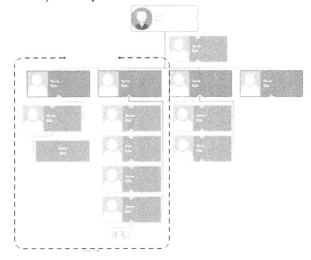

39. Select the second left Manager shape and enter Paul in the **Name** field on the **SHAPE DATA** window.
40. Select the Manager shape with the name Paul and click **ORG CHART > Layout > Synchronize > Create Synchronized Copy**.

41. On the **Create Synchronized Copy** dialog, select the **New page** option and check the **Hide subordinates on the original** page.
42. Click **OK**. A new page is created and the Manager and his subordinates are moved to it.

43. Click the **Page-1** tab located below the drawing page.

Notice that the subordinates of the Manager are hidden.

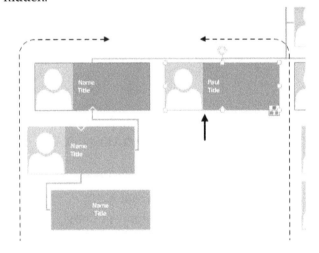

44. Right-click on the Manager shape with the name Paul and select **Hyperlink** .

45. On the **Hyperlinks** dialog, click the **Browse** button next to the **Sub-address** box.

46. On the **Hyperlink** dialog, select **Page-2** from the **Page** drop-down, and click **OK**.

47. Enter **Subordinates page** in the **Description** box and click **OK**.

48. Press the Ctrl key and click on the Manager shape with the hyperlink. The Page-2 is opened.

49. Drag the Staff Notch shape and drop it on the lower most Position shape.

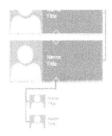

50. On the Page-2, right click on the Manager shape and select **Hyperlink**.

51. On the **Hyperlinks** dialog, click the **Browse** button next to the **Sub-address** box.

52. On the **Hyperlink** dialog, select **Page-1** from the **Page** drop-down, and click **OK**.

53. Enter **Return to top** in the **Description** box and click **OK**.

54. Right click on the Manager shape and select **Return to top**. The main page is opened.

55. Select the Manager shape with the name Paul and click **ORG CHART > Arrange > Show/Hide Subordinates** to display the subordinates.

56. Right click on the lower most Position of the synchronized Manager shape and select **Subordinates > Synchronize Subordinates**. The subordinates under the Position are synchronized.

# Tutorial 7 (Creating Organizational Charts using Wizard)

1. Start Visio 2013.
2. On the Backstage, click the **Business** Category and select the **Organizational Chart Wizard** template.

Organization Chart Wizard

3. Select the **US Units** and click **Create**.
57. On the **Organization Chart Wizard** dialog, select the **Information that I enter using Wizard** option, and click **Next**. If you have the information stored in a file, then select the **Information that's already stored in a file or database** option.
58. Select the **Excel** option and click **Browse**. You can also use the **Delimiter text** option to create a file in which the data is separated by a comma or space.
4. Go to a location on your drive and type-in **OrgCharWizardExample** and click **Save**.
5. Click **Next**. A message box appears asking you to type over the sample text, save and close the file.
6. Click **OK**. An excel file is opened and notice the sample data in it. You can modify or add data to it.
7. Type-in the data in the sixth row, as shown.

| | Name | Reports_to | Title | Department | Telephone |
|---|---|---|---|---|---|
| 1 | | | | | |
| 2 | | | | | |
| 3 | Joe Sampleboss | | CEO | Executive | x5555 |
| 4 | Jane Samplemgr | Joe Sampleboss | Development Manager | Product Development | x6666 |
| 5 | John Samplepos | Jane Samplemgr | Software Developer | Product Development | x6667 |
| 6 | Anna | Joe Sampleboss | Software Developer | Product Development | x6668 |

8. Click the **Save** button on the Quick Access Toolbar and close Microsoft Excel.
9. Select **Don't include pictures in my organization chart**, and click **Next**. You can also use the **Locate the folder that contains your organization pictures** option to specify the folder in which the pictures are located.
10. Examine the options displayed on the last page. Most of them are self-explanatory.
11. Leave the default settings and click **Finish**.
12. Zoom-in to the diagram.

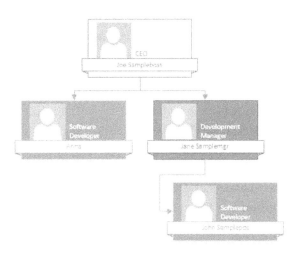

# Tutorial 8 (Creating Organizational Charts using External Data)

1. Download the OrgCharWizardExample2.xlsx file and open it.

| | Name | Manager | Title | Department | Telephone | Performance | Master_Shape |
|---|---|---|---|---|---|---|---|
| 1 | Name | Manager | Title | Department | Telephone | Performance | Master_Shape |
| 2 | | | | | | | |
| 3 | Fred Acton | | CEO | Executive | 235-0256 | 8 | |
| 4 | Beth Cameron | Fred Acton | Executive Assistant | Office of CEO | 235-0257 | 9 | Assistant |
| 5 | Lord Calvin | Fred Acton | Administrative Head | Administration | 235-0258 | 7 | |
| 6 | Charles Edward | Fred Acton | Investigation Director | Investigation | 235-0259 | 8 | |
| 7 | Kirk Meister | Fred Acton | Services Manager | Support Service | 235-0260 | 7 | |
| 8 | Dave Anke | Fred Acton | Uniforms | Uniforms | 235-0261 | 9 | |
| 9 | Guy Michaels | Charles Edward | Detective Manager | Investigation | 235-0262 | 8 | |
| 10 | Bruce Franks | Kirk Meister | Records | Support Service | 235-0263 | 6 | |
| 11 | Todd Fuller | Lord Calvin | Professional Standards | Administration | 235-0264 | 8 | |
| 12 | Judy Grant | Charles Edward | Gang Task Force | Investigation | 235-0265 | 9 | |
| 13 | Alex Jong | Dave Anke | Special Operations | Uniforms | 235-0266 | 7 | |
| 14 | Alan Koons | Kirk Meister | Information | Support Service | 235-0267 | 6 | |
| 15 | John Mero | Dave Anke | Patrol Section | Uniforms | 235-0268 | 9 | |
| 16 | Nayla Olson | Kirk Meister | Quartermaster | Support Service | 235-0269 | 8 | |
| 17 | George Patrick | Lord Calvin | Narcotics | Administration | 235-0270 | 5 | |
| 18 | Karl Ray | Charles Edward | Family Protection | Investigation | 235-0271 | 7 | |
| 19 | Joan Ruskin | Kirk Meister | System Administration | Support Service | 235-0272 | 8 | |
| 20 | Babe Shinoda | Dave Anke | Traffic Section | Uniforms | 235-0273 | 6 | |
| 21 | Joseph Stein | Kirk Meister | Security Officer | Support Service | 235-0274 | 9 | |
| 22 | Lily Tucker | Lord Calvin | Planning and Research | Administration | 235-0275 | 8 | |
| 23 | Jack Waless | Charles Edward | Forensics | Investigation | 235-0276 | 8 | |
| 24 | Martha Waugh | Dave Anke | Mounted Patrol | Uniforms | 235-0277 | 9 | |
| 25 | Elie Wilson | Kirk Meister | Vehicle maintenance | Support Service | 235-0278 | 9 | |
| 26 | Wilbur Young | Lord Calvin | Crime Analyst | Administration | 235-0279 | 8 | |
| 27 | Emile Twain | Charles Edward | Special Detail | Investigation | 235-0280 | 7 | |

Notice the first row on the Spreadsheet. It has various columns such as Name, Title, Manager, Department, and Telephone. You can also add more columns to this row. The cells below the first row has all the data of the organization. The **Name** column shows the name of the employee and the Manager column shows the manager to whom the employee reports. For example, Lord Calvin (Administrative head) reports to Fred Acton (CEO). Make sure that the name, spelling, and casing of the manager is same as that shown in the Name column.

Also, notice the **Master_Shape** column in the spreadsheet. The Assistant shape is assigned for Beth Cameron, who is the Executive Assistant of the CEO. By default, Visio assigns the Manager shape to all the employees reporting to the CEO. You can assign a shape to an employee in the Master_Shape column.

2. Close the Excel file.
3. Start Visio 2013.
4. On the Backstage, click the **Business** Category and select the **Organizational Chart** template.
5. Select the **US Units** and click **Create**.
6. On the ribbon, click **DESIGN > Backgrounds > Backgrounds > Flow**.

7. On the ribbon, click **ORG CHART > Organization Data > Import** .
8. On the **Organization Chart Wizard** dialog, select the **Information that's already stored in a file or database** option, and click **Next**.
9. Select the **A text, Org Plus (*.txt), or Excel file** option and click **Next**.
10. Click the **Browse** button and go to a location of **OrgCharWizardExample2** file and double click on it.
11. Click **Next**.
12. Make sure that **Name** is set to **Name** and **Reports to** is set to **Manager**.
13. Click **Next**.

Now, you can select the data fields to be displayed on the shapes. By default, the Name and Title information is displayed. You can add more data by selecting them from the **Data file columns** section and clicking the **Add** button. If you do not want to display the data field on the shape, then select it from the **Data fields** section and click the **Remove** button.

14. Click **Next**.
15. Press the Ctrl key and Select all the data fields from the Data file columns section except the Master_shape data field.

16. Click the **Add** button to add it to the **Shape Data field** section. The data fields displayed in the **Data field** section will be added to the shape. You can see this data on the **SHAPE DATA** Window.
17. Click **Next**.
18. Select **Don't include pictures in my organization chart**, and click **Next**.
19. Select the **I want to specify how much of my organization to display on each page** option.
20. Leave the **Hyperlink employee shapes across pages** and **Synchronize employee shapes across pages** options checked.
21. Click **Next**.
22. Click the **Add Page** button on the dialog.
23. Select **Lord Calvin** and **All Subordinates** from the **Name at top of page** and **Number of additional levels** drop-downs, respectively.
24. Click **OK**.
25. Likewise, add three more pages of managers and click **Finish**.

| Employee at Top of Page | Additional Levels | Page Nam |
|---|---|---|
| Fred Acton | All Subordinates | |
| Lord Calvin | All Subordinates | |
| Charles Edward | All Subordinates | |
| Kirk Meister | All Subordinates | |
| Dave Anke | All Subordinates | |

Notice that five pages are created.

26. On the Page-5, select all the shapes and click **ORG CHART > Layout > Layout > Side by Side > Single Side**.
27. Click **Best Fit to Page** on the **Layout** group.
28. Likewise, change the layouts on Page-2, Page-3, and Page-4.
29. Click the **Page-1** tab below the drawing page. The entire organization chart is displayed.
30. Select the four managers under the CEO one-by-one and click the **Show/Hide Subordinates** on the ribbon. The organization chart is collapsed a little-bit.

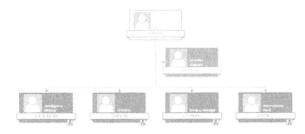

31. Place the pointer on any of the Manager shapes and notice the Hyperlink glyph.
32. Press the Ctrl key and click on the **Investigation Director** shape. Separate page is opened with the manager and his subordinates.

33. Press Ctrl and click on the **Investigation Director** to go back to **Page-1**.
34. Select the **Investigation Director** shape and click **INSERT > Links > Hyperlink**.
35. On the **Hyperlinks** dialog, click in the **Sub-address** box and delete the **/Sheet.1** text.
36. Enter **Investigation team** in the **Description** box and click **OK**.
37. Select the **Investigation Director** shape and click **DATA > Show/Hide > Shape Data Window**. The data related to the selected shape is displayed.

| Department | Investigation |
| --- | --- |
| Telephone | 235-0259 |
| Name | Charles Edward |
| Title | Investigation Direc |
| Manager | Fred Acton |
| Performance | 8 |

## Link Data to Shapes

Earlier you have learned to create a diagram using an external database. However, there will be a situation where the database is modified. For this purpose, Visio allows you to relink the diagram to data so that it is updated, automatically.

1. On the ribbon, click **DATA > External Data > Link Data to Shapes** .
2. On the **Data Selector** dialog, select the **Microsoft Excel workbook** option, and click **Next**.
3. Click the **Browse** button and go to a location of **OrgCharWizardExample2** file and double click on it.
4. Click **Next**.
5. Click the **Select Custom Range** button.
6. Drag a box covering all the data on workbook and click **OK**.

7. Leave the **First row of data contains column headings** option checked and click **Next**.
8. Click the **Select Columns** button and uncheck the **Master_Shape** option.
9. Click **OK**.
10. Click **Next**.
11. Leave the **Name** column checked. The values entered in the **Name** column will be used to identify the data in the data table.
12. Click **Next** and **Finish**. Notice the external data table displayed in the lower portion of the window. The data in the table is not linked to shapes in the diagram. You can link the data manually or automatically.

13. On the drawing page, zoom to the CEO shape.
14. Drag the **Fred Acton** cell from the data table and release on the CEO shape.

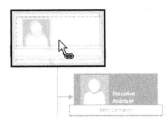

The data graphics appears next to the CEO shape. Also, the link symbol appears next to Fred Acton cell in the data table. This is the manual method to link data to the diagram. However, it is a tedious process if you have a large data.

Visio provides you with an option to link data to the diagram, automatically.

15. On the ribbon, click **DATA > External Data > Automatically Link** .
16. Leave the **All shapes on this page** option selected and click **Next**.
17. Select **Name** from the **Data Column** and **Shape field** drop-downs.
18. Click **Next** and **Finish**. Notice the links symbols in the data table and the data graphics on the drawing page.

19. Click on the drawing page and press Ctrl+A.
20. On the ribbon, click **DATA > Display Data > Data graphics > No Data Graphic**. The Data graphics are hidden

Use the **Refresh All** command on the **DATA** tab of the ribbon to update the diagram whenever you change the database.

You can also click **Refresh All > Refresh Data** on the **DATA** tab of the ribbon to configure the data refresh. On the **Refresh Data** dialog, click the **Configure** button to open the **Configure Refresh** dialog.

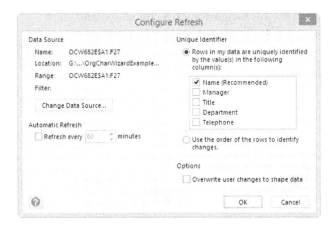

On the **Configure Refresh** dialog, you can set the refresh time by checking the **Refresh every** option and entering the duration. Note that if you add a new record to the data, it will not be reflected in the diagram. If you delete a record from the database, the shape related to it will be empty in the diagram. Also, if you move an employee from one manager and place him under another, you have to update the diagram manually.

## Creating Data Graphics

Data graphics help you to represent a specific information of a shape in a graphical way.

1. Close the **External Data Window** by unchecking the **External Data Window** on the **DATA** tab of the ribbon.
2. On the **DATA** tab of the ribbon, click **Display Data > Data graphics > Create New Data Graphic**.
3. Click **New Item**.
4. On the **New Item** dialog, select **Data field > Department**.
5. Select **Displayed as > Color by Value**. Notice the color assignments for each department. If you notice two color assignments for the Administration department, select one of them and click the **Delete** button. You can change the fill and text colors of the departments using the **Fill Color** and **Text Color** drop-downs.

6. Click **OK** twice.
7. Press Ctrl+A to select all the shapes.
8. On the **DATA** tab of the ribbon, click **Display Data > Data graphics > Data Graphic**.

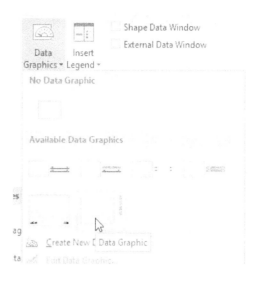

9. On the **DATA** tab of the ribbon, click **> Display Data > Insert Legend > Vertical**.

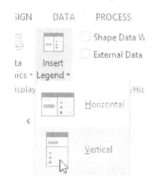

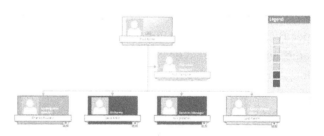

10. On the **DATA** tab of the ribbon, click **Display Data > Data graphics**.
11. On the **Data graphics** drop-down, right click on the previously created data graphics and select **Edit**.
12. Click **New Item**.
13. On the **New Item** dialog, select **Data field > Performance**.
14. Select **Displayed as > Icon Set**.
15. Select the default Style.

16. Set the **Rules for showing each icon** options, as shown.

17. Select **Horizontal > Right**, and **Vertical > Top**.
18. Click **OK** twice. The performance of the employees indicated by the data graphics.

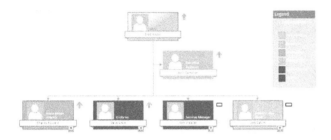

## Exporting the Chart to PDF format

1. Click **FILE > Save As > Browse**.
2. Select **Save as type > PDF**.
3. Specify the location of the PDF file, enter the File name, and click **Save**. The PDF file is created along with hyperlinks.

## Publishing to Web page format

1. Click **FILE > Save As > Browse.**
2. Select **Save as type > Web page**.
3. Specify the location of the html file, enter the File name, and click **Save**. The HTML file is created along with a folder.
4. Open the HTML file, if not already opened.

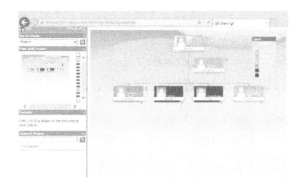

You can select a page number from the **Go To Page** drop-down and click the arrow button next to it. The selected page will be opened.

You can drag a box in the **Pan and Zoom** section to zoom to a particular portion of the diagram.

Press the Ctrl key and click on any shape to view the data related to it.

# Tutorial 9 (Creating Pivot Diagrams)

1. Download the **PivotDiagramExample.xlxs** file.
2. Start Visio 2013.
3. On the Backstage, click the **Business** Category and select the **PivotDiagram** template.

PivotDiagram

4. Select the **US Units** and click **Create**.
5. On the **Data Selector** dialog, select **Microsoft Excel Workbook**, and click **Next**.
6. Click the **Browse** button.
7. Go to a location of the **PivotDiagramExample.xlxs** file and double click on it.
8. Click **Next**.
9. Click the **Select Custom Range** button.

10. Drag a box covering all the data on workbook and click **OK**.

11. Leave the **First row of data contains column headings** option checked and click **Next**.
12. Click **Next**.
13. Click **Finish**. Notice the Top node of the Pivot diagram on the drawing page. Also, the information about the data source is displayed. The Top node displays the total of the Performance in the organization.

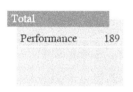

14. On the PivotDiagram window, uncheck the **Performance** option, and check the **Count** option under the **Add Total** section.
15. On the PivotDiagram window, click **Add Category > Department** (or) right click on the top node and select **Add Category > Department**. The **Department** category is added to the diagram.

16. Select the **Administration** node from the drawing page and click **Add Category > Manager** on the PivotDiagram window (or)

right click on the **Administration** node and select **Add Category > Manager**. The **Manager** category is added under the Administration node.

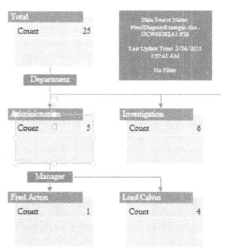

17. Select the **Administration** node from the drawing page and click **PIVOT DIAGRAM > Layout > Direction > Left to Right**.

The direction of the Managers is changed to Left-to-Right. Select a different option on the Direction drop-down and notice the difference.

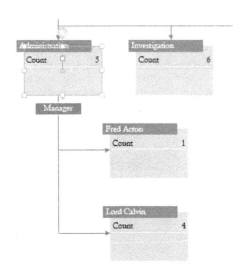

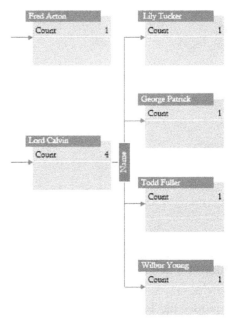

18. Select the **Lord Calvin** node from the drawing page and click **PIVOT DIAGRAM > Layout > Direction > Left to Right**.
19. On the PivotDiagram window, click **Add Category > Name** with the **Lord Calvin** node selected.
20. Select the **Lord Calvin** node from the drawing page and click **PIVOT DIAGRAM > Layout > Alignment > Middle**.

The alignment of the employees under Lord Calvin is changed to Middle. You can also set a different type of alignment using the **Alignment** drop-down. Note that the Center and Right options are effective when the Direction is set to Top-to-Bottom or Bottom-to-Top.

21. Select the **Name** breakdown and click **PIVOT DIAGRAM > Sort & Filter > Sort & Filter**.
22. Select **Descending** and click **OK**. Notice that the order of the name is changed.
23. Select the **Department** breakdown and click **PIVOT DIAGRAM > Sort & Filter > Filter**.
24. On the **Configure Column** dialog, select **Show data where Department > does not end with**.
25. Type CEO in the box next to the drop-down, and click **OK**. The **Office of CEO** node is removed from the Department breakdown.

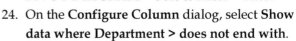

26. Select the **Lord Calvin** node from the drawing page and click **PIVOT DIAGRAM > Arrange > Collapse** (or) right click on **Lord Calvin** and select **Collapse**. The employees under **Lord Calvin** are collapsed.
27. Click the **Undo** icon on the Quick Access Toolbar (or) press Ctrl+Z.
28. Press the Ctrl key and select the four employees under Lord Calvin.

29. On the ribbon, click **PIVOT DIAGRAM >**

    **Arrange > Merge** 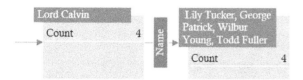. The four employees are merged together into single node.

30. Select the merged node and click **PIVOT DIAGRAM > Arrange > Unmerge** on the ribbon. The merged node is split.

31. Press Ctrl and select all the four employees under **Lord Calvin**.

32. On the PivotDiagram window, click **Add Category > Telephone**. The telephone nodes are added to the four employees.

33. Select the Lily Tucker node and click **PIVOT DIAGRAM > Format > Apply Shape** .

34. On the **Apply Shape** dialog, select **Stencil > Workflow Objects**.

35. Select the **User** shape and click **OK**.

The User shape is added to the selected node.

36. Drag a selection box across the other three employees under Lord Calvin and click **PIVOT DIAGRAM > Format > Apply Shape** .

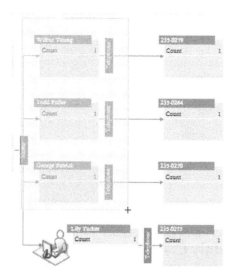

37. On the **Add Shape** dialog, select **Stencil > Workflow Objects**.

38. Select the **User** shape and click **OK**.

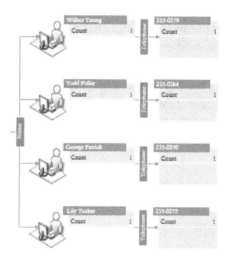

Likewise, you can add other shapes to different nodes.

You can link text data to the shapes using the **Link Data to Shapes** command available on the DATA tab of the ribbon.

# Tutorial 10 (Creating Calendars)

1. Start Visio 2013.
2. On the Backstage, click the **Schedules** Category and select the **Calendar** template.

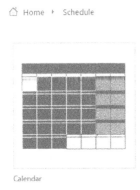

Home ▸ Schedule

Calendar

3.  Select the **US Units** and click **Create**.

## Creating Monthly Calendars

1.  On the Shapes Window, select the **Month** shape, drag and drop it on the drawing page.
2.  On the **Configure** dialog, set the **Month** to **February.** Also, set the **Year**, **Begin week on**, and **Language** settings.
3.  Set **Shade weekends** to **Yes** and click **OK**. The Calendar is centered on the drawing page, automatically.
4.  Click and drag the top right corner of the calendar to reduce its size.
5.  Drag the calendar to the lower middle portion of the drawing page.

6.  On the Shapes Window, select the **Thumbnail Month** shape, drag and drop it on the top left corner of the drawing page.

7.  On the **Shape Data** dialog, select **Month > 01-January**, and click **OK**.
8.  Drag another Thumbnail Month and position it on the top right corner.

9.  On the **Shape Data** dialog, select **Month > 03-March**, and click **OK**.
10. Right click on the **Page-1** tab located below the drawing page and select **Duplicate**. A page is created along with calendars.

Insert
Delete
Rename
Duplicate
Page Setup...
Reorder Pages...

Page

11. Right click on the large calendar and select **Configure**.

12. On the **Configure** dialog, select **Month > March,** and click **OK**.
13. Click **OK** on the **Calendar** message box.
14. Likewise, change the top left and top right calendars to February and April, respectively.
15. Right click on the Page-1, select **Rename**, and type-in **February**.
16. Likewise, rename the Page-2 tab as March.

February    March    All ▲    ⊕

## Adding Appointments, Multi-day events, Texts to Calendars

1. On the Shapes Window, select the **Appointment** shape, drag and drop it on the calendar.

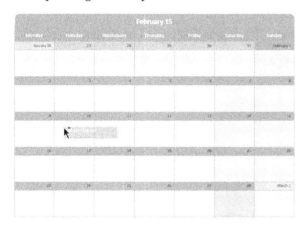

2. On the **Configure** dialog, set the **Start time**, **End time**, **Subject, Location, Time format** and **Date**.
3. Click **OK** to add the appointment. You can revise the appointment by right clicking on it and selecting **Configure**.

4. On the Shapes Window, select the **Multi-day events** shape, drag and drop it on the calendar.

5. On the **Configure** dialog, enter the subject and set the **Start time**, **End time**, and **Location**.
6. Click **OK** to add the event.

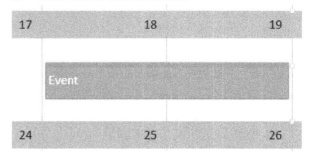

7. Double-click in a day of the calendar and type-in text.
8. Press Esc to exit the text box. Note that you need to select the text and change its color for some themes.

## Adding Calendar Art Shapes

1. On the Shapes Window, select the **Meeting** Art shape, drag and drop it on the calendar.
2. Resize and position the art shape to fit into a day.

Likewise, you can add other art shapes available on the Shapes window. For example, you can add the **Travel-air** art shape to show the air travelling schedule.

Note that the art shapes are not associated with an event or appointment. If you change an event date, you need move the art shape, manually.

## Creating Daily Calendars

1. Click **Insert Page** at the bottom of the drawing page.
2. On the Shapes Window, select the **Day** shape, drag and drop it on the drawing page.
3. On the **Configure** dialog, set the Date or leave it as current date.
4. Set the **Language** and **Date format**, and click **OK**.

You can change the Date and date format by right clicking on the calendar and selecting **Configure**.

## Creating Weekly Calendars

1. Click **Insert Page** at the bottom of the drawing page.
2. On the Shapes Window, select the **Week** shape, drag and drop it on the drawing page.
3. On the **Configure** dialog, specify the **Start date**.
4. Specify the **End date** by selecting the number of days from the **End date** drop-down.
5. Set the **Language** and **Date format**, and then specify **Yes** or **No** for **Shaded weekend**.
6. Click **OK**.

If you want to create a Multi-Week calendar, then drag the **Multi-week** shape onto the drawing page. Specify the Start date, End date and other settings and click **OK**.

You can also import **Outlook Data** into Visio Calendar drawing by using the **Import Outlook Data** command on the **CALENDAR** tab of the ribbon.

# Tutorial 11 (Creating Timelines)

Timelines are used to represent the tasks and deadlines in a timeline manner.

1. Start Visio 2013.
2. On the Backstage, click the **Schedule** Category and select the **Timeline** template.

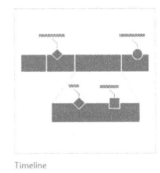

Timeline

3. Select the **US Units** and click **Create**.
4. On the Shapes Window, select **Cylindrical timeline**, drag and drop it on the drawing page. You can also use the **Block timeline**, or **Line timeline** as they all the same except the appearance.
5. On the **Configure Timeline** dialog, set the **Start** date to 1/1/2015 and **Finish** date to 12/31/2015.
6. Leave the **Time scale** to **Months**.
7. Click the **Time Format** tab and set the **Date Formats** to Month name (ex: Feb).
8. Click **OK**.

9. On the Shapes Window, select the **Triangle milestone**, drag and drop it between the Jan and Feb interval.

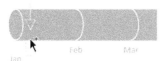

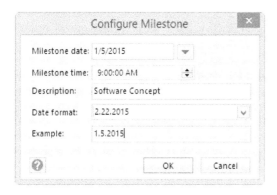

10. Specify the settings on the **Configure Milestone** dialog, as shown.

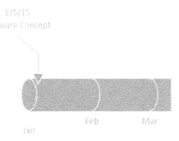

11. Click **OK**.

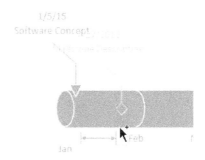

12. On the Shapes Window, select the **Diamond milestone**, drag and drop it between the Jan and Feb interval.

13. Specify the settings on the **Configure Milestone** dialog, as shown.

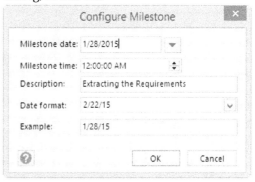

14. Click **OK**. The texts of the milestone overlap.

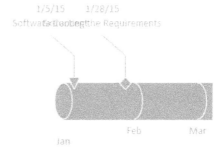

15. Click and drag the horizontal guide, and then release it, as shown.

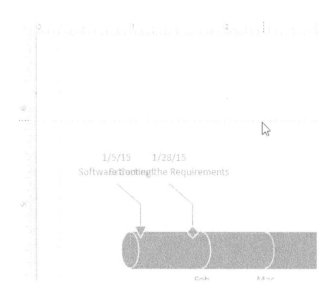

16. Select the second milestone.
17. Drag the **Reposition Text** handle and glue it to the guide.

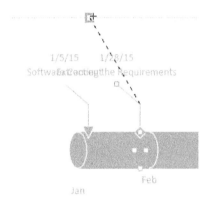

If you want to edit a milestone, select it and click **TIMELINE > Milestone > Configure**. Modify the settings on the **Configure Milestone** dialog and click **OK**.

18. On the Shapes Window, select the **Block interval**, drag and drop it between the **May** and **Aug** interval.

19. Specify the settings on the **Configure Interval** dialog, as shown.

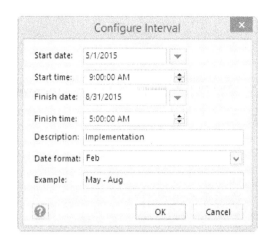

20. Click **OK**.

If you want to edit an interval, select it and click **TIMELINE > Interval > Configure**. Modify the settings on the **Configure Interval** dialog and click **OK**.

21. Create other milestones (Diamond, Line, Square, and X milestones) on the timeline, as shown.

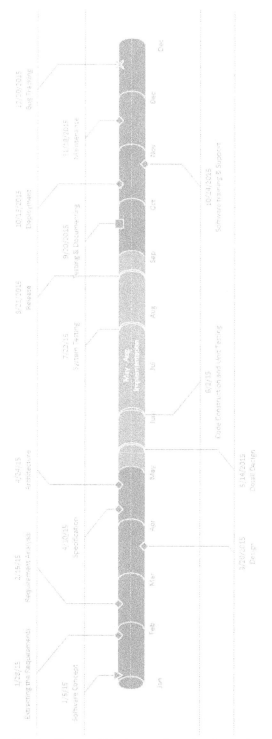

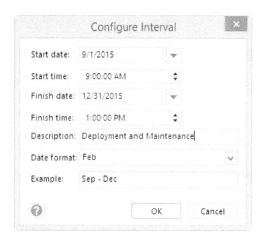

24. Drag the text handle of the Curly bracket and glue it to the lower most guide.

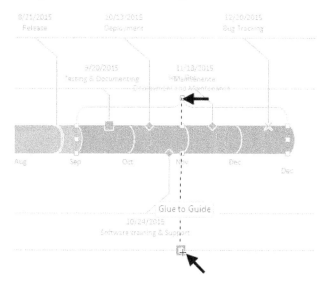

25. Drag the other handle of the curly bracket and snap it to the lower most guide.

22. On the Shapes Window, select the **Curly bracket interval** shape, drag and drop it on the timeline.
23. Specify the settings on the **Configure Interval** dialog, as shown.

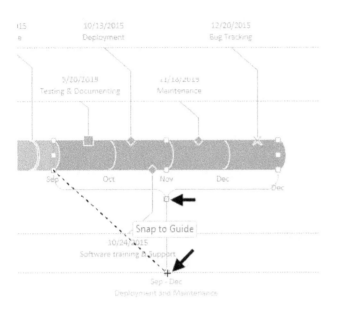

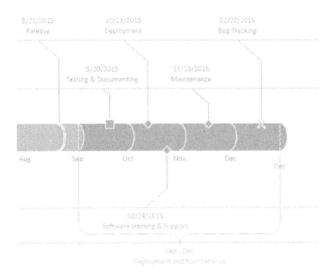

26. On the Shapes Window, select the **Today marker** shape, drag and drop it on the timeline. The marker is placed on the current date. The position of the marker will change daily to reflect the current date.

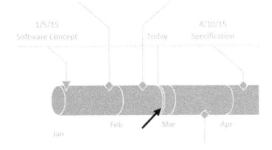

27. On the Shapes Window, select the **Elapsed time** shape, drag and drop it on the timeline. The marker is placed between the starting of the timeline and the current date.

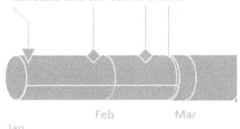

28. On the Shapes Window, select the **Expanded timeline** shape, drag and drop it on lower portion of the drawing page.
29. On the **Configure Timeline** dialog, set the **Start** and **Finish** dates to 5/1/2015 and 8/31/2015, respectively.
30. Set **Time scale** to **Weeks** and click **OK**.

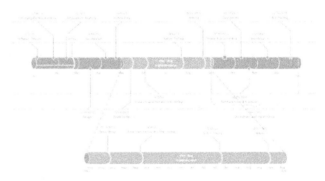

You can change the expanded timeline size by dragging the dashed lines attached to main timeline.

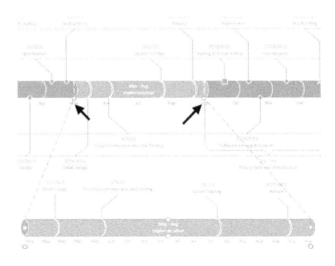

You can also add milestones to the expanded timeline.

If you have Microsoft Project installed on your computer, you can export timelines to a Microsoft Project file using the **Export Data** command available on the **TIMELINE** tab of the ribbon.

You can also import a Microsoft Project file into Visio using the **Import Data** command on the **TIMELINE** tab of the ribbon.

# Tutorial 12 (Creating Detailed Network Diagrams)

1. Start Visio 2013.
2. On the Backstage, click the **Network** Category and select the **Detailed Network Diagram-3D** template.

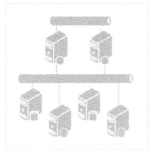

Detailed Network Diagram - 3D

3. Select the **US Units** and click **Create**.
4. On the Shapes Window, select the **Ethernet** shape, drag and drop it on the drawing page.

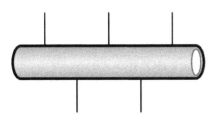

5. Select the end point of the upper middle connector and drag it to the right.

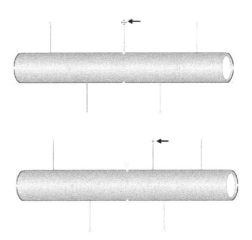

6. On the ribbon, click **HOME > Tools > Connector**.
7. Click on the Ethernet shape, drag the pointer up, and release it to create a connector.

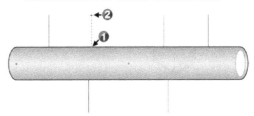

8. Likewise, add two connectors, as shown.

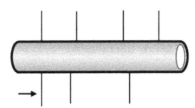

9. On the Shapes Window, select the **Network and Peripherals-3D** stencil.
10. Select the **Multi-function device** shape, drag and drop it below the **Ethernet** shape.
11. Select the **Pointer Tool** icon from the **Tools** group of the ribbon.
12. Resize the **Multi-function device**.
13. On the ribbon, click **View > Show > Task Pane > Size & Position**.

14. Select the shape and modify the Width on the **SIZE & POSITION** pane to 0.3 in.

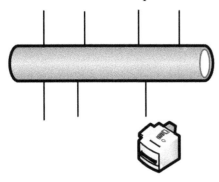

15. On the Shapes Window, select the **Scanner** shape, drag and drop it below the Ethernet shape.

16. On the Shapes Window, select the **Copier** shape, drag and drop it below the Ethernet shape.

17. Resize the Scanner and Copier shapes.

18. On the Shapes Window, select the **Computers and Monitors-3D** stencil.

19. On the Shapes Window, select the **PC** shape, drag and drop it above the Ethernet shape.

20. Resize the PC shape.

21. Press the Ctrl key and drag the PC shape to duplicate it.

22. Likewise, create two more PC shapes.

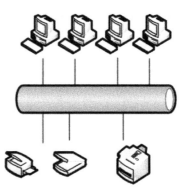

23. Drag the end point of the connector and glue it to the **Multi-function** device.

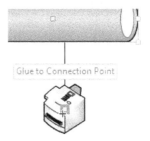

24. Likewise, glue other connectors to the remaining shapes, as shown.

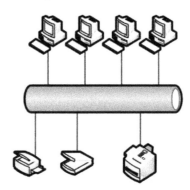

25. Select the Copier, Scanner, and Multi-function device.

26. On the ribbon, click **HOME > Arrange > Position > Distribute Horizontally** .

27. Likewise, distribute the PC shape horizontally.

**Microsoft Visio 2013 Basics**

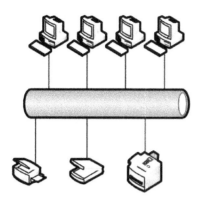

28. Select the Copier, Scanner, and Multi-function device.
29. On the ribbon, click **HOME > Arrange > Align > Align Bottom** .
30. Select all the PC shapes and click **HOME > Arrange > Align > Align Top** .
31. Drag a selection box covering all the shapes.
32. Drag the Resize handle located at the bottom right corner to increase the size of all the shapes.

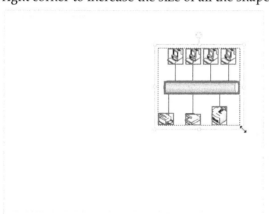

33. On the ribbon, click **INSERT > Diagram Parts > Container > Classic**.

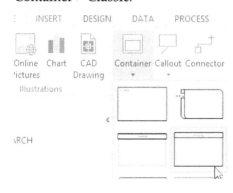

The container encloses all the shapes. Also, the **CONTAINER TOOLS FORMAT** tab appears on the ribbon. On this tab, you can define the container size and style settings.

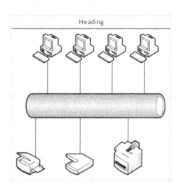

34. Type **Office Network** and press Esc.
35. Drag the container and position it on the left side of the drawing page.

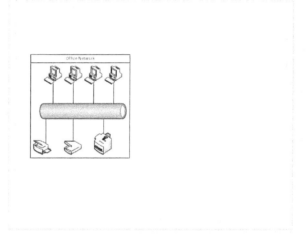

36. On the Shapes Window, select the **Network and Peripherals-3D** stencil.
37. On the Shapes Window, select the **Firewall** shape, drag and drop it on the drawing page.
38. On the ribbon, click **HOME > Tools > Connector**.
39. Select the connection point of the container, as shown.

40. Drag the pointer and glue to the connection point of the Firewall shape.

41. On the Shapes Window, select the **Router** shape, drag and drop it next to the Firewall shape.

You can also go to *http://www.cisco.com/c/en/us/products/visio-stencil-listing.html* and download more stencils. To open them in Visio, click **More Shapes > Open Stencil** on the Shapes Window.

42. On the Shapes Window, select the **Wireless access point** shape, drag and drop it above the Router shape.
43. Connect the Firewall, Router, and Wireless access point.

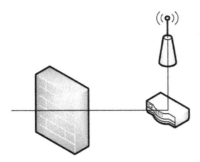

44. Select the connectors and click **HOME > Arrange > Send to Back** on the ribbon.
45. Click the SEARCH tab on the Shapes Window and type-in internet in the search bar.

46. On the Shapes Window, select the **Cloud** shape, drag and drop it next to the Router.
47. Select the **Pointer Tool** icon on the **Tools** group of the ribbon.
48. Select the Cloud shape and type-in Internet. Press Esc.

49. Click the **STENCILS** tab on the Shapes Window.
50. On the Shapes Window, select the **Network and Peripherals-3D** stencil.
51. On the Shapes Window, select the **Comm-link** shape, drag and glue to the Cloud.

52. On the Shapes Window, select the **Network and Peripherals-3D** stencil.
53. On the Shapes Window, select the **Dynamic Connector** shape, drag and glue to the Firewall shape.

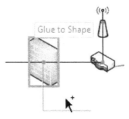

54. Drag the midpoint of the connector.

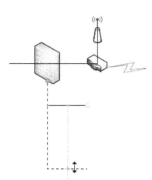

55. On the Shapes Window, select the **Smart phone** shape, drag and drop it on the drawing page.
56. On the Shapes Window, select the **Computers and Monitors** stencil.
57. On the Shapes Window, select the **Laptop Computer** shape, drag and drop it on the drawing page.

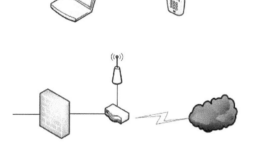

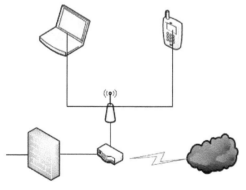

58. Create two connectors from the **Wireless access point** to Smart phone and Laptop Computer.
59. Select the **Pointer Tool** icon on the **Tools** group of the ribbon.
60. Select the connectors and click **HOME > Arrange > Send to Back** on the ribbon.

61. Right click on the connectors and select **Straight Connectors**.
62. Select both the connectors and click **HOME > Shape Styles > Line > Line Options**.
63. On the **Format Shape** pane, select **Dash Type > Dot**.

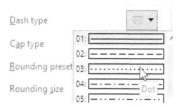

The connectors are converted to dotted lines.

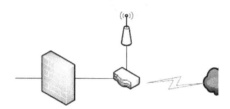

64. On the ribbon, click **HOME > Tools > Rectangle**.
65. Create a rectangular shape at the bottom right corner.
66. Type-in Database in the rectangular shape.
67. Select all the text by pressing Ctrl+A.
68. On the HOME tab of the ribbon, change the **Font Size** to 24 pt.
69. Drag the end point of the connector and glue it to the rectangular shape.

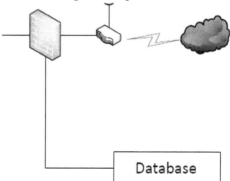

70. Select the rectangular shape and click **PROCESS** > **Subprocess** > **Create New** 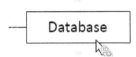.

71. Place the pointer on the rectangular shape and notice the hyperlink glyph. The rectangular links to Page-2.

Database

72. Press the Ctrl key and click to navigate to Page-2.

73. On the Shapes Window, select the **Network and Peripherals-3D** stencil.

74. On the Shapes Window, select the **Ring Network** 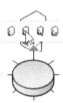 shape, drag and drop it at the center of the drawing page.

75. Place the pointer on the Ring network.

76. Place the pointer on the arrow pointing upwards, and select the **File Server** shape.

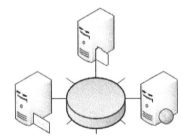

77. Likewise, add the **Email Server** and **Web Server** shapes.

78. On the Shapes Window, select the **Servers-3D** stencil.

79. Drag the **Database Server** shape from the Server-3D stencil, and drop it below the Round Network.

80. Create a connection between the Round network and Database Server.

81. Select the connector and click **HOME** > **Arrange** > **Send to Back** on the ribbon.

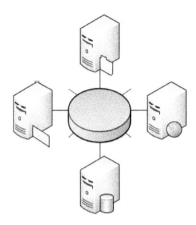

82. Select the **Round Network** shape and drag the end point of the connector, as shown.

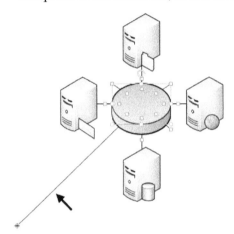

83. Create a rectangular shape a4nd hyperlink it to the Page-1.

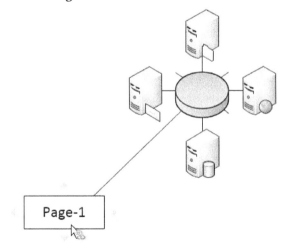

You can link text data to the shapes using the **Link Data to Shapes** command available on the **DATA** tab of the ribbon.

You can also use the **Data Graphics** command to add data graphics to the shapes and modify them.

# Index

www.ingramcontent.com/pod-product-compliance
Lightning Source LLC
Chambersburg PA
CBHW060206060326
40690CB00018B/4273